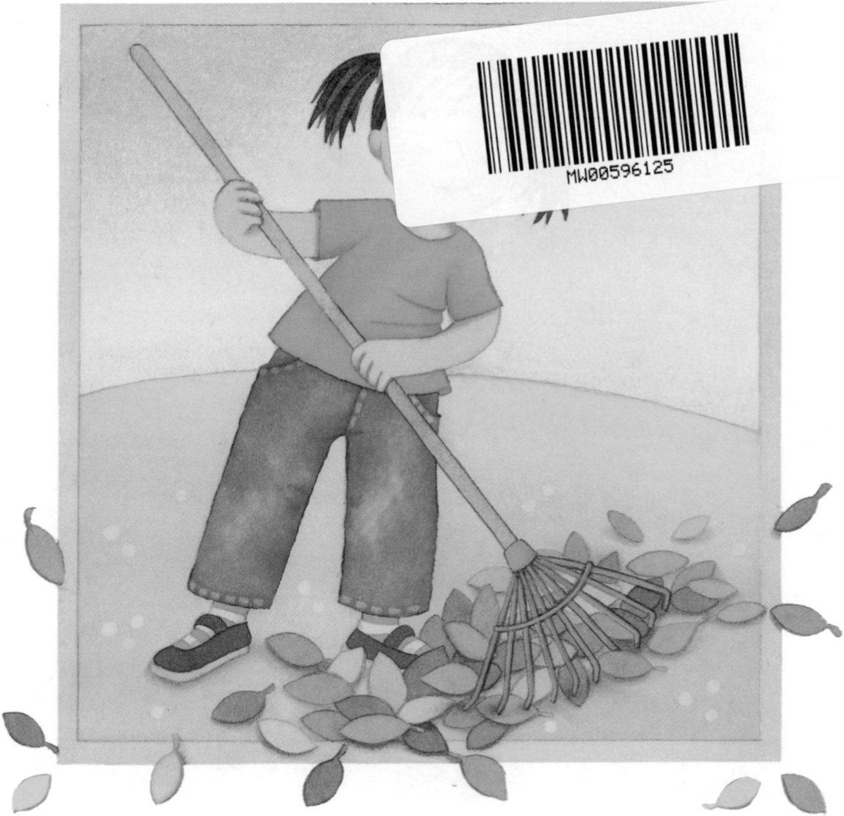

I rake

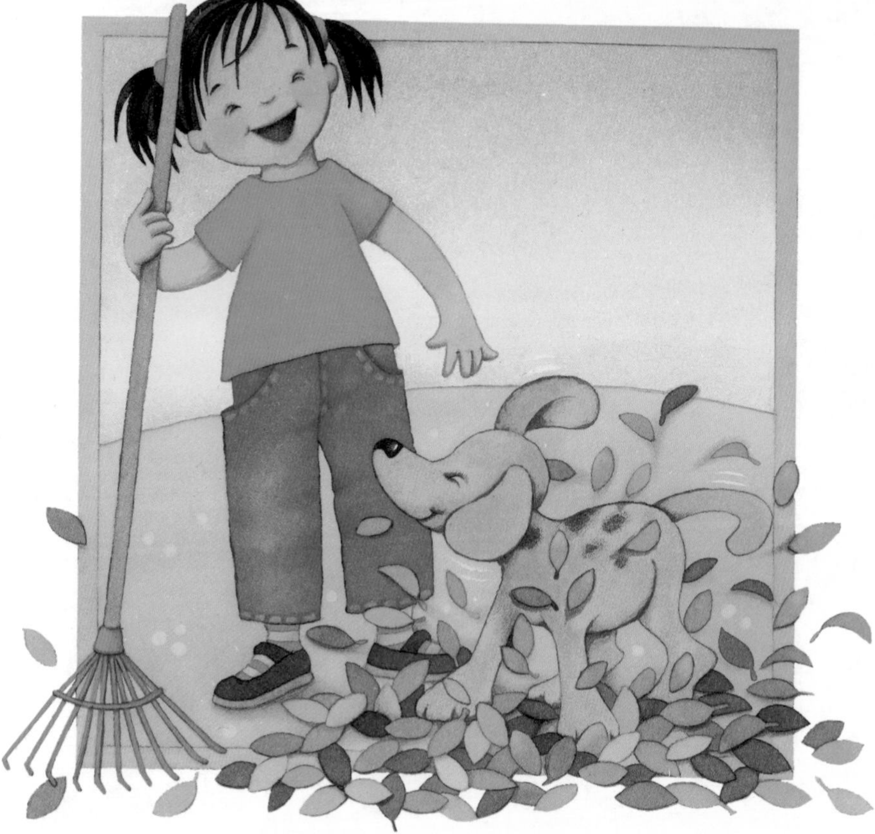

and you shake.

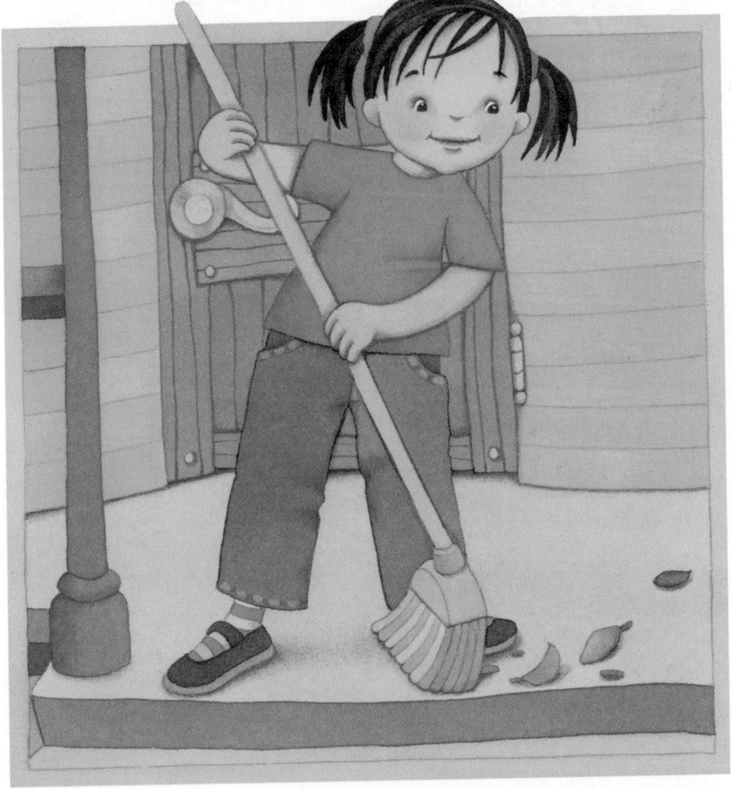

I sweep

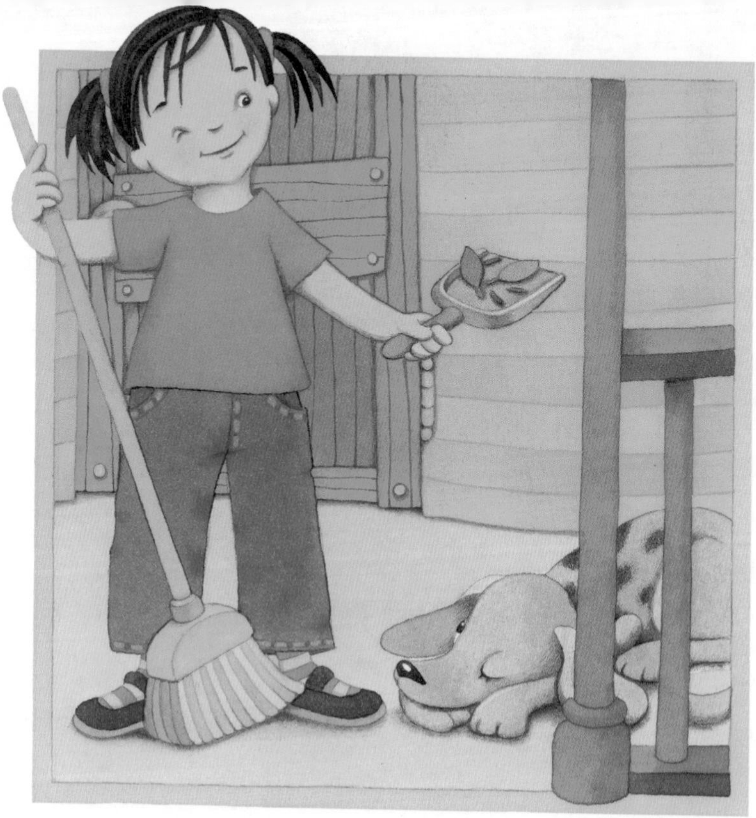

and you sleep.

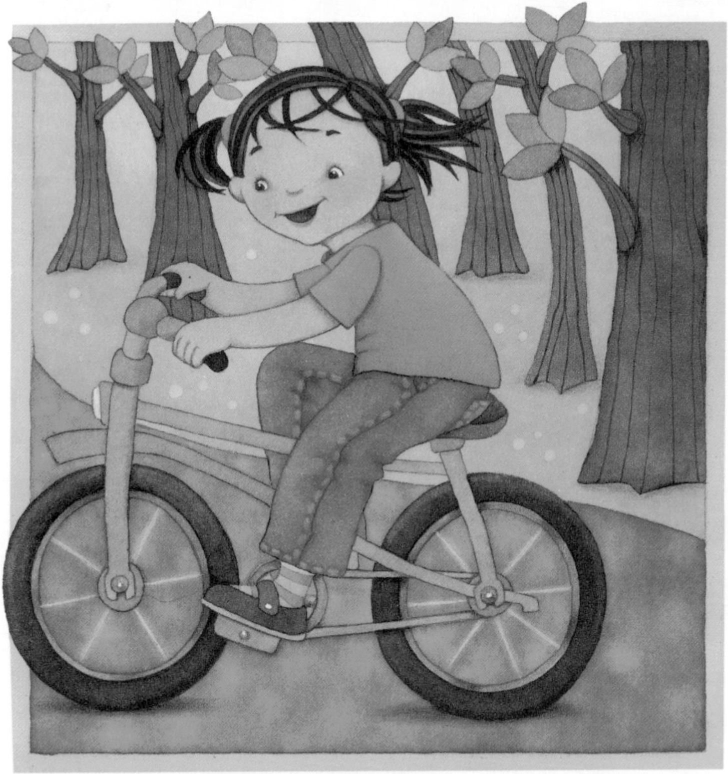

I ride

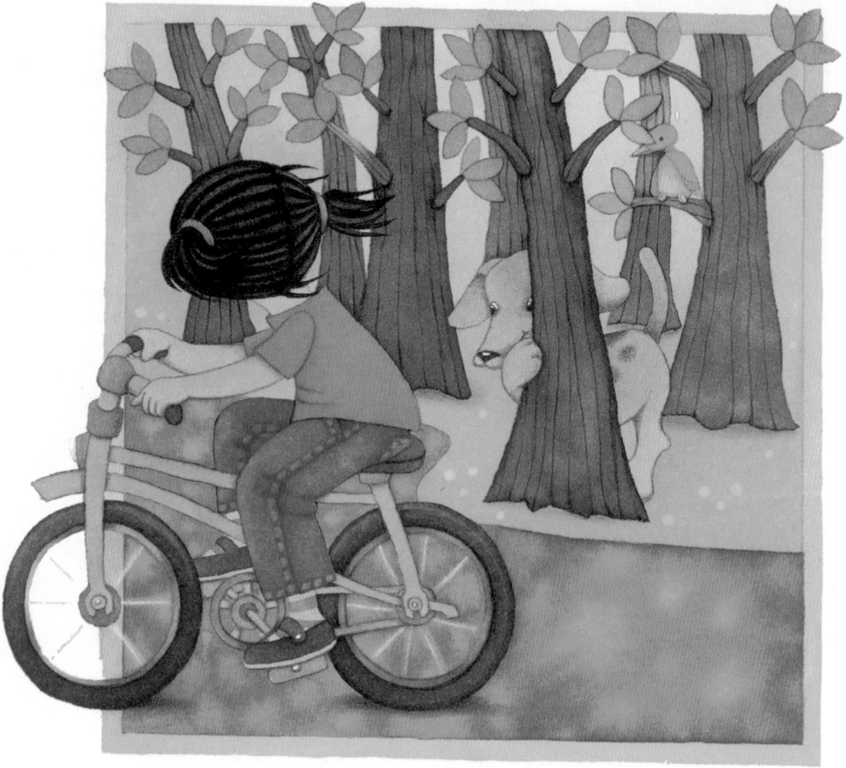

and you hide.

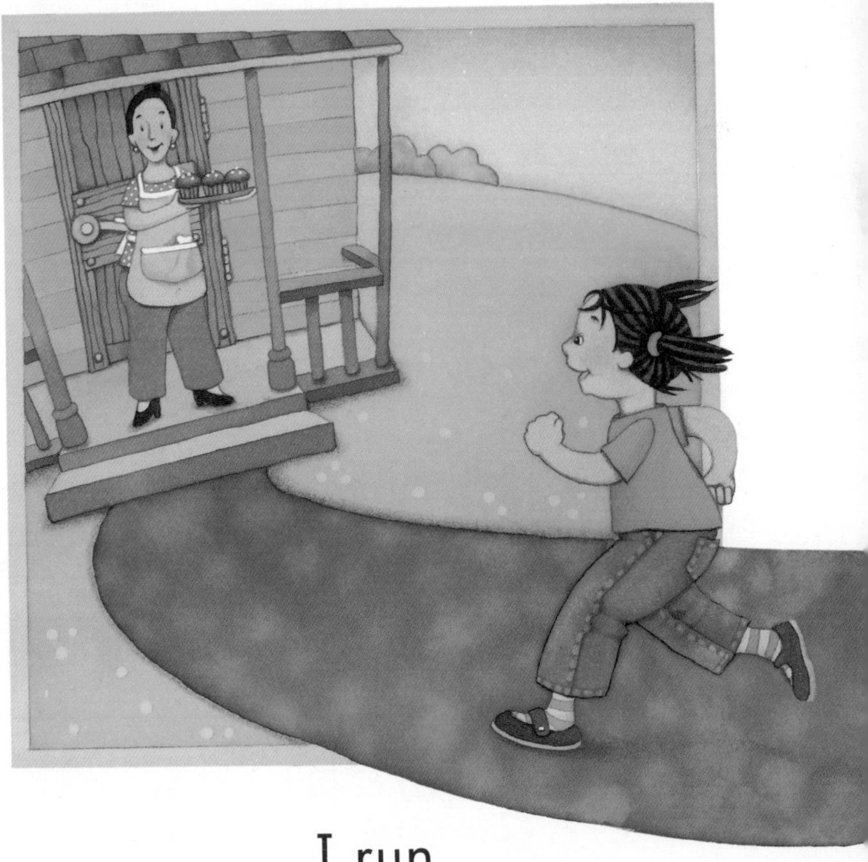

I run

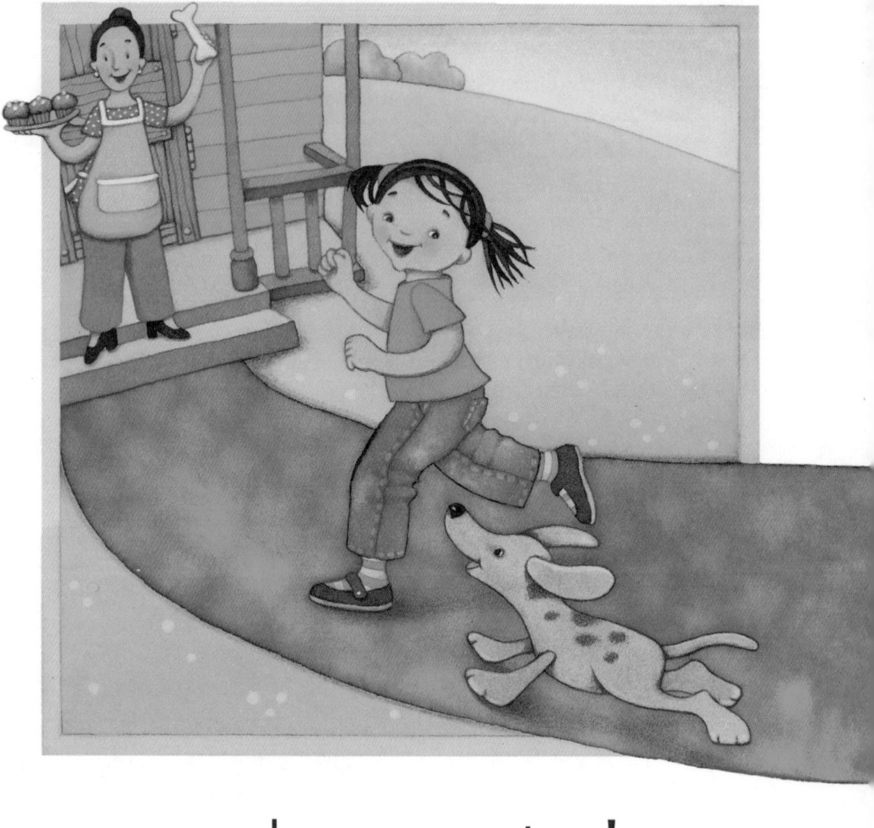

and you run too!